I0494584

Butt Ends and Banana Slugs

Lyle Rosbotham

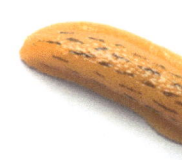

© 2013 Lyle Rosbotham
ISBN 978-0-917796-00-5

Press Four Fifty One
SAN: 262-0707
www.lylerosbotham.com

Cover drawing by Joan Wolbier

These photographs were taken on the Quinault Loop Trail
on the south side of Lake Quinault in Olympic National Forest.

For more information:
www.fs.usda.gov/recarea/olympic/recreation/recarea/?recid=47769&actid=50
www.wta.org/go-hiking/hikes/quinault-rain-forest-loop

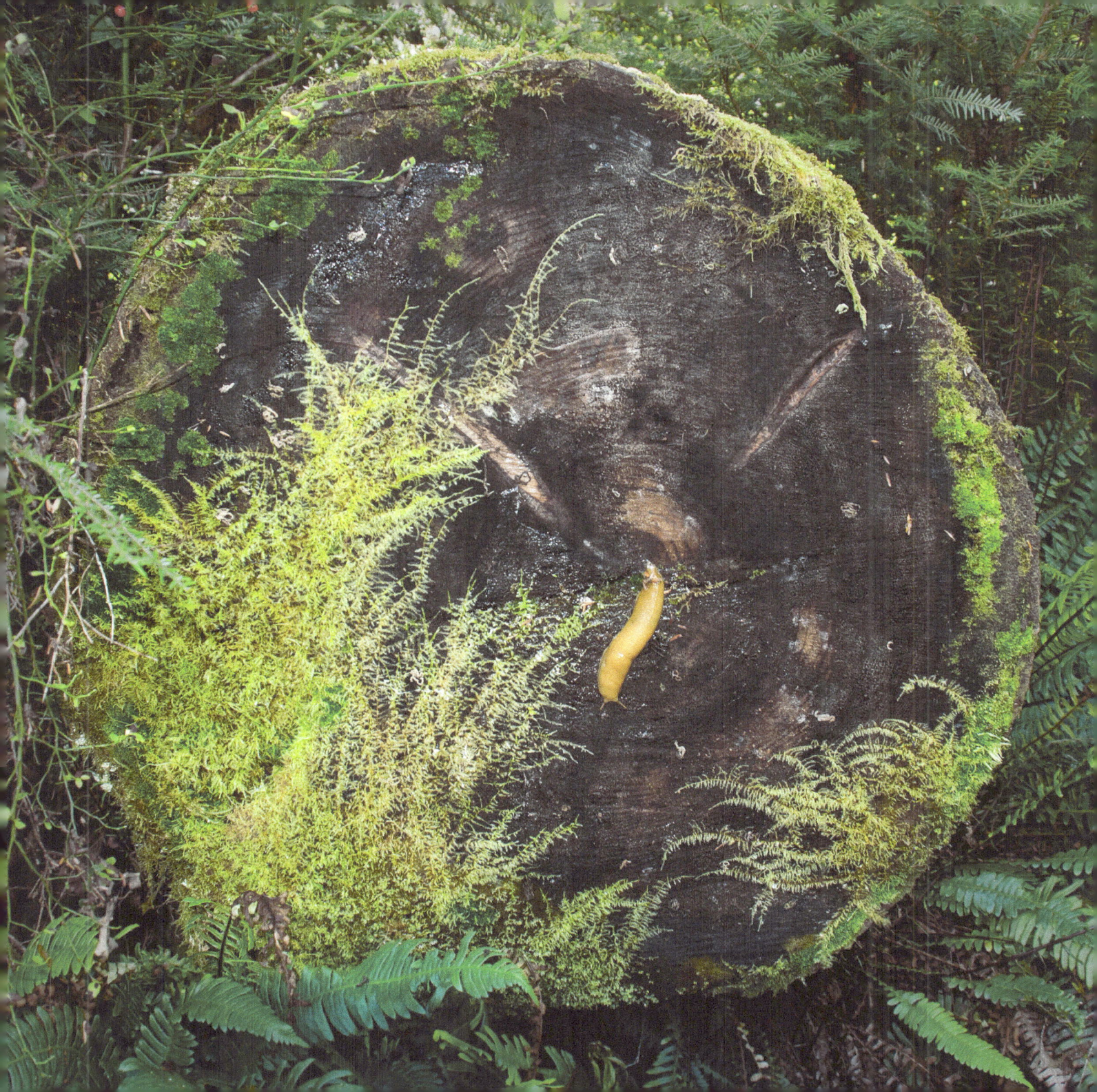

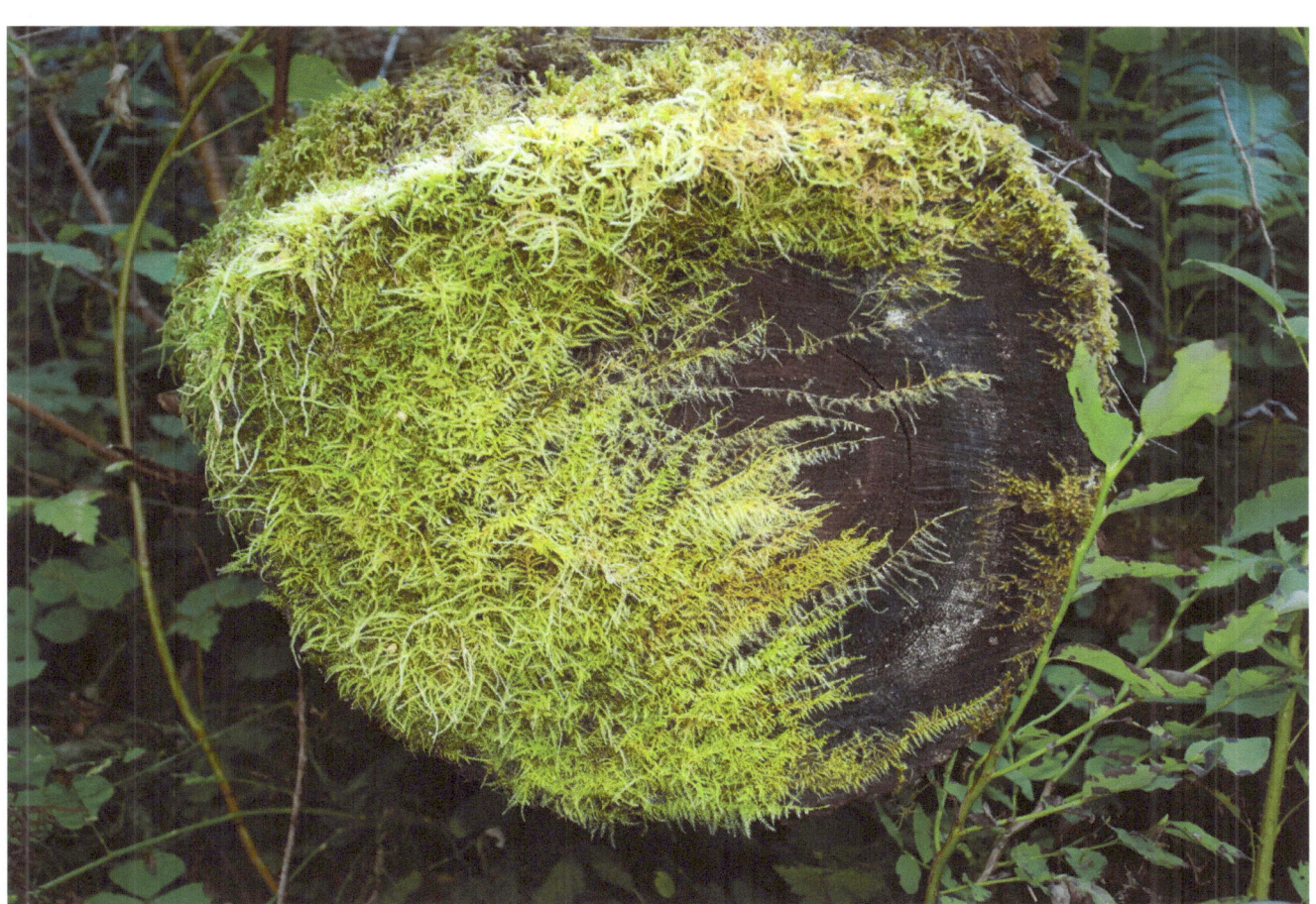

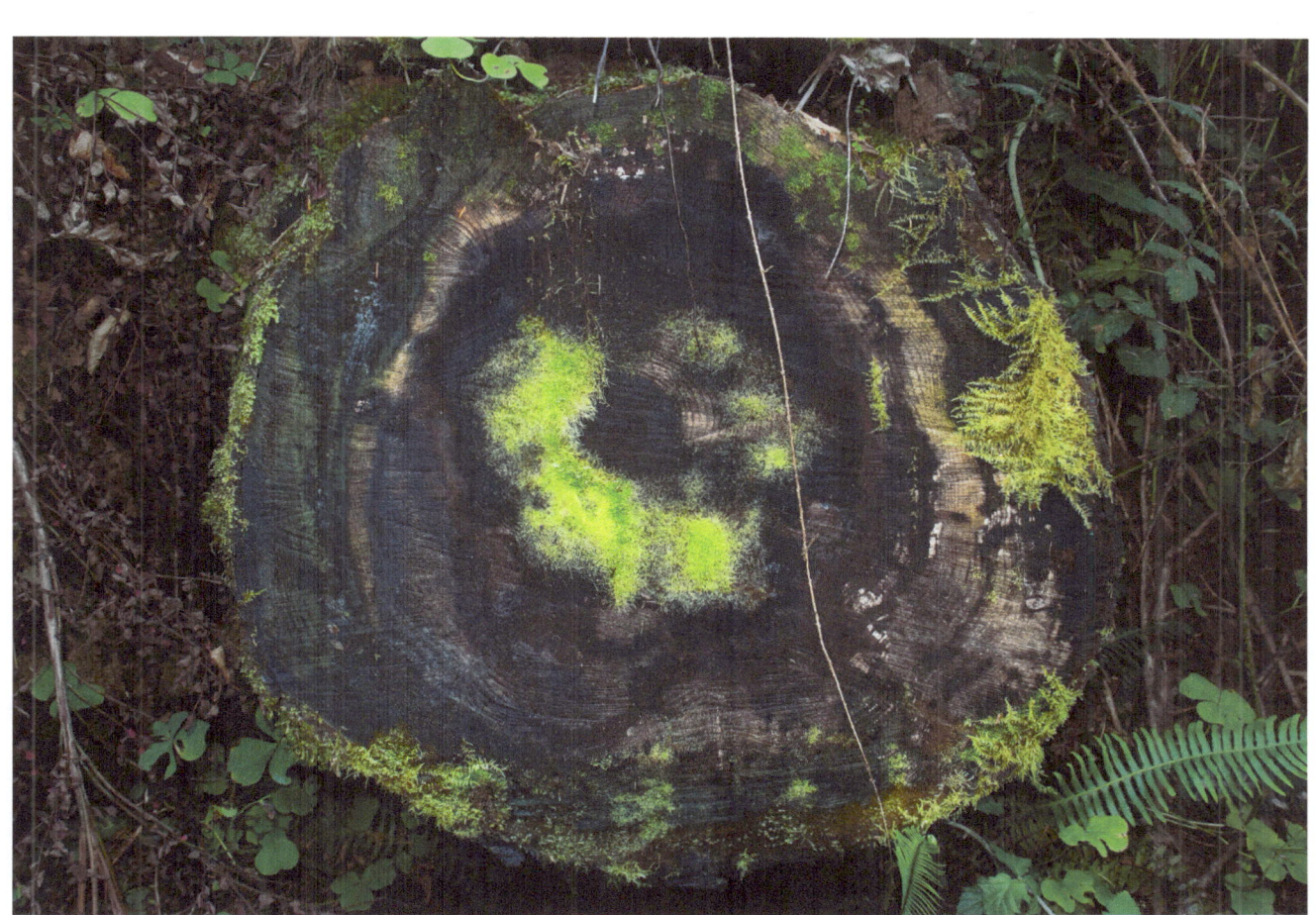

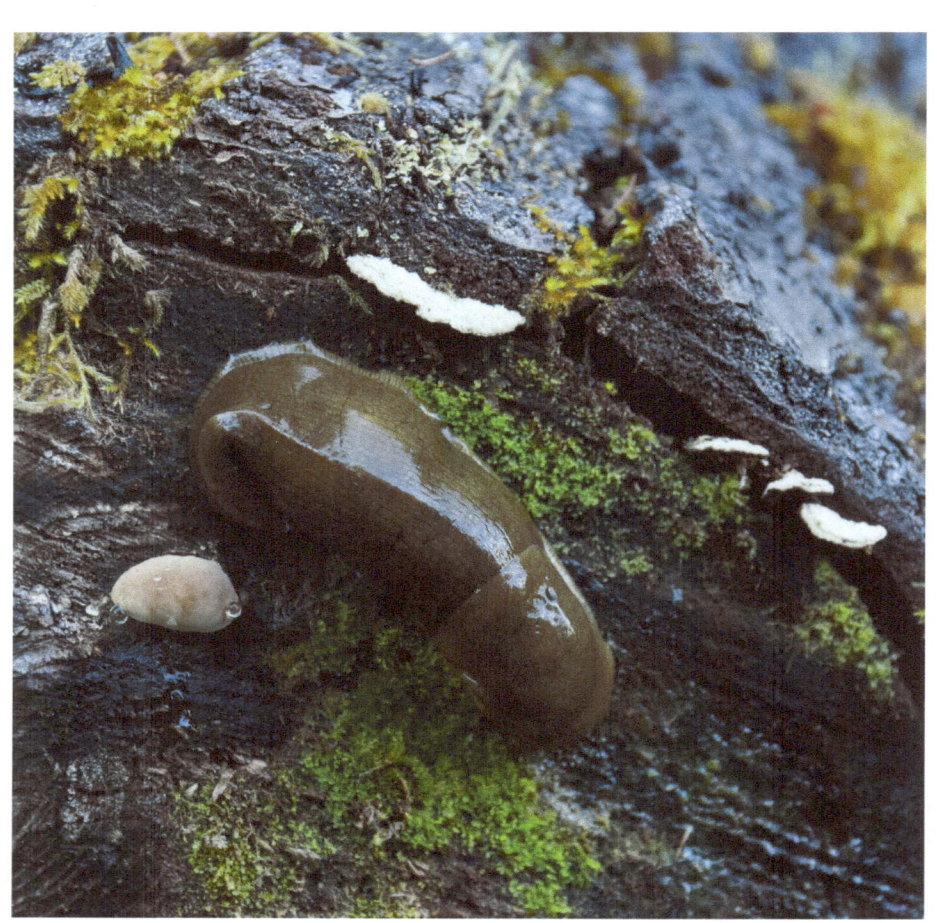

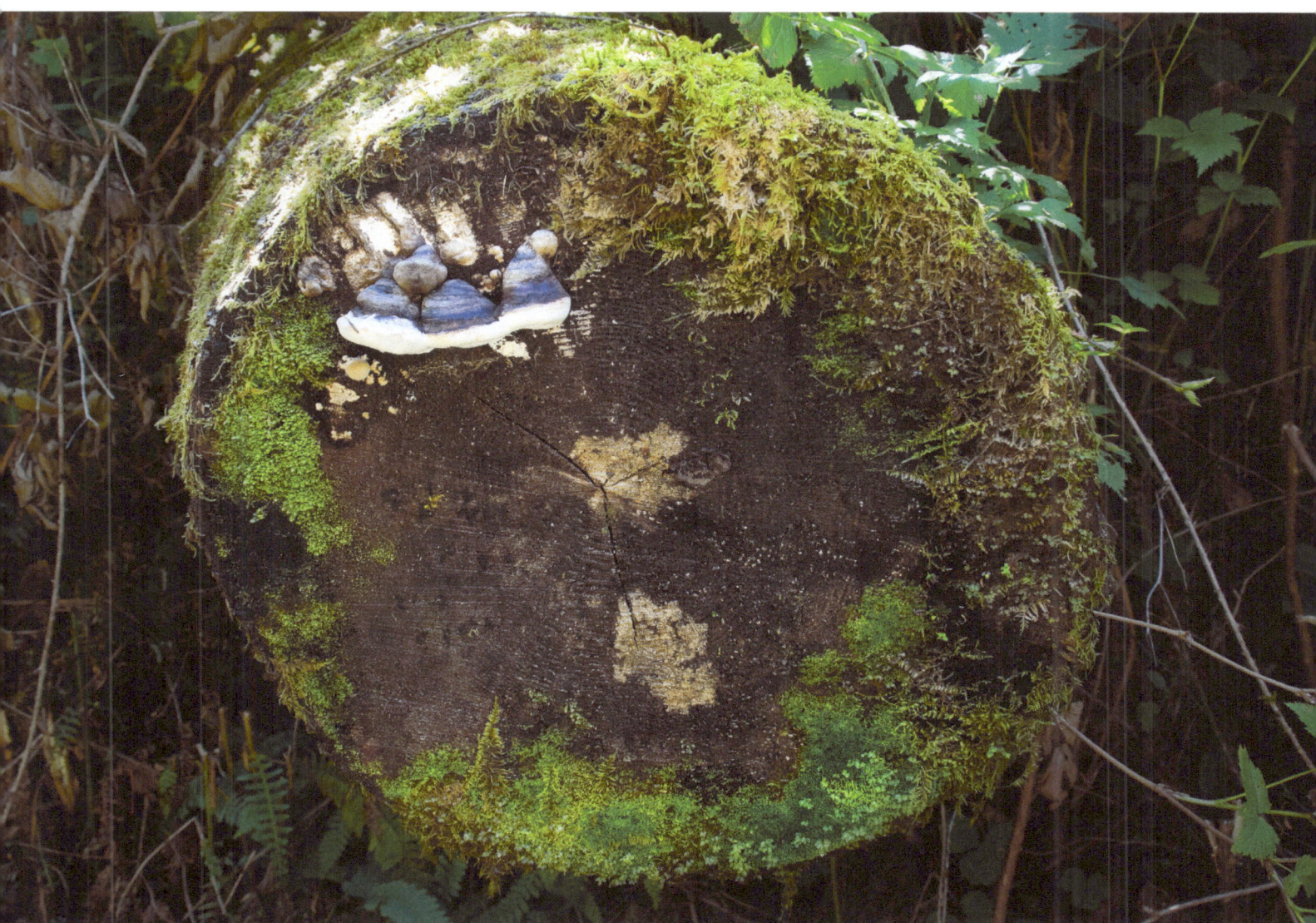

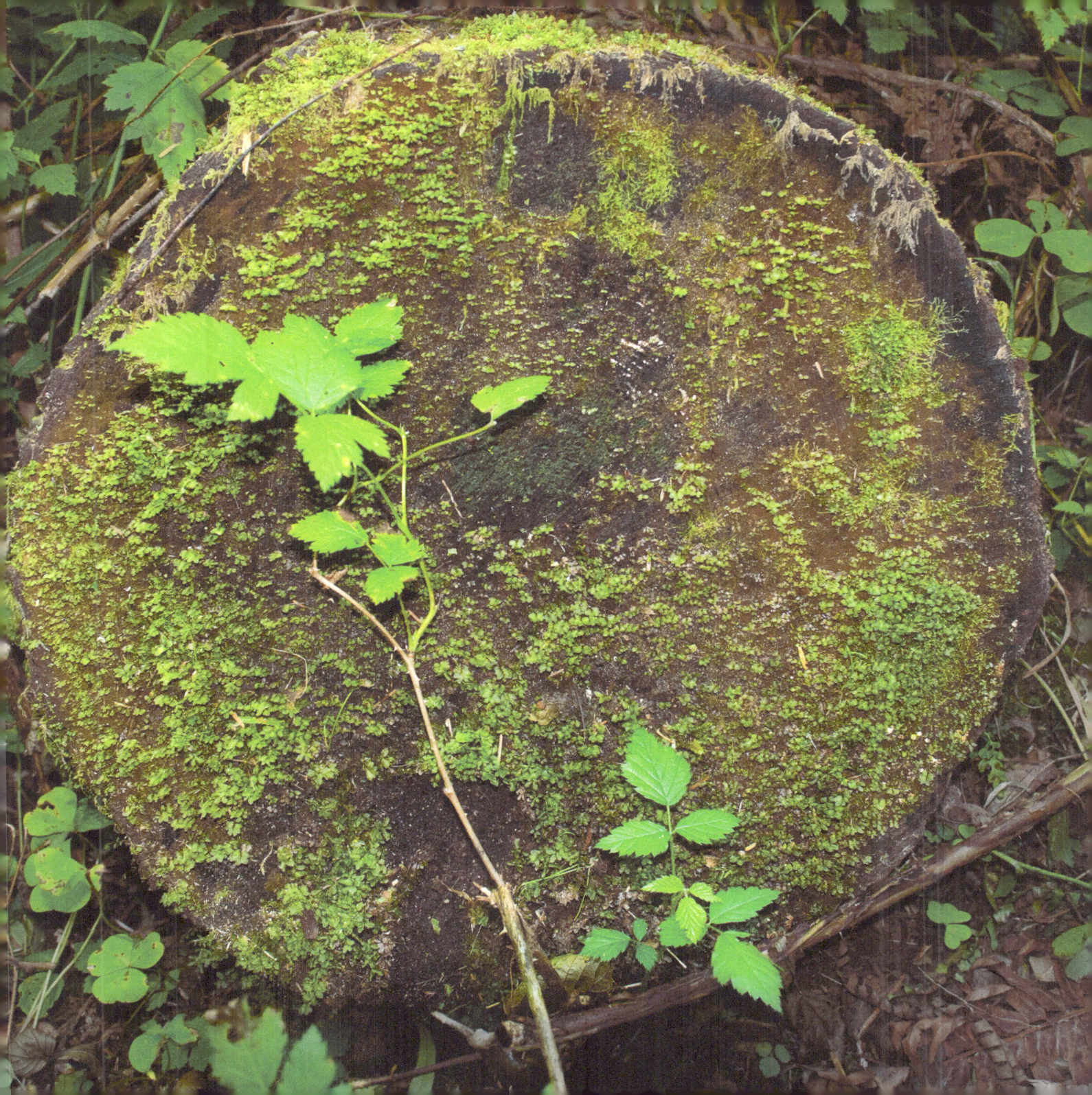

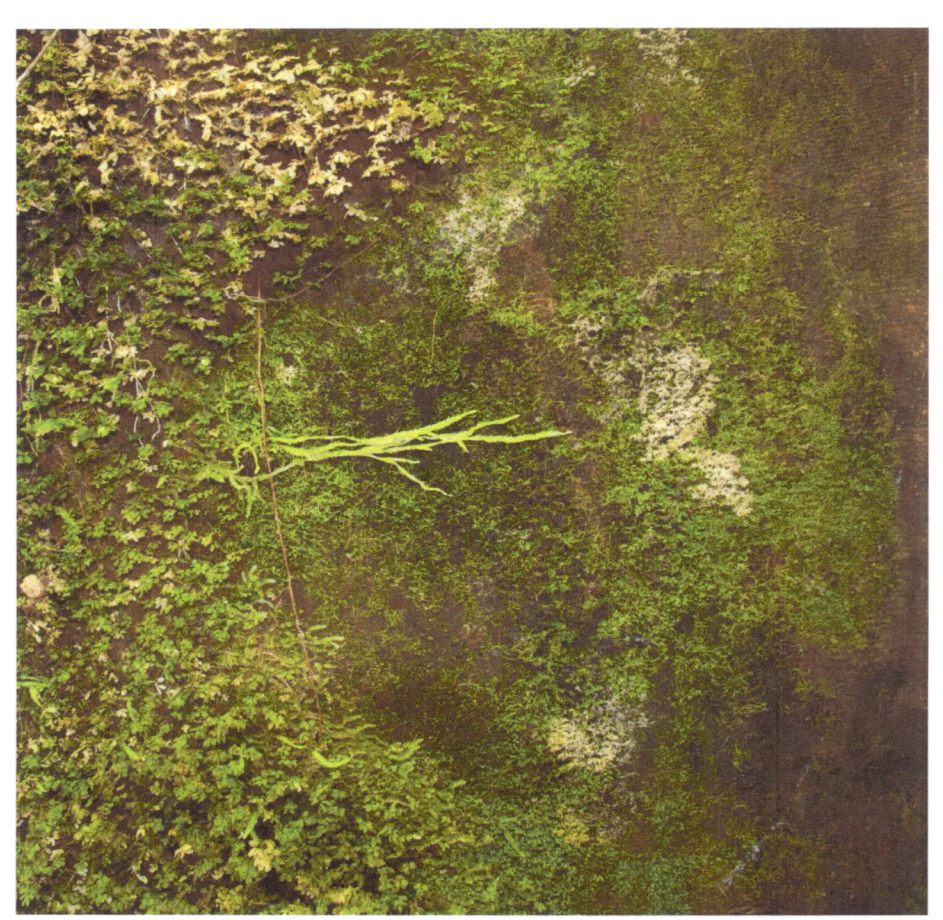

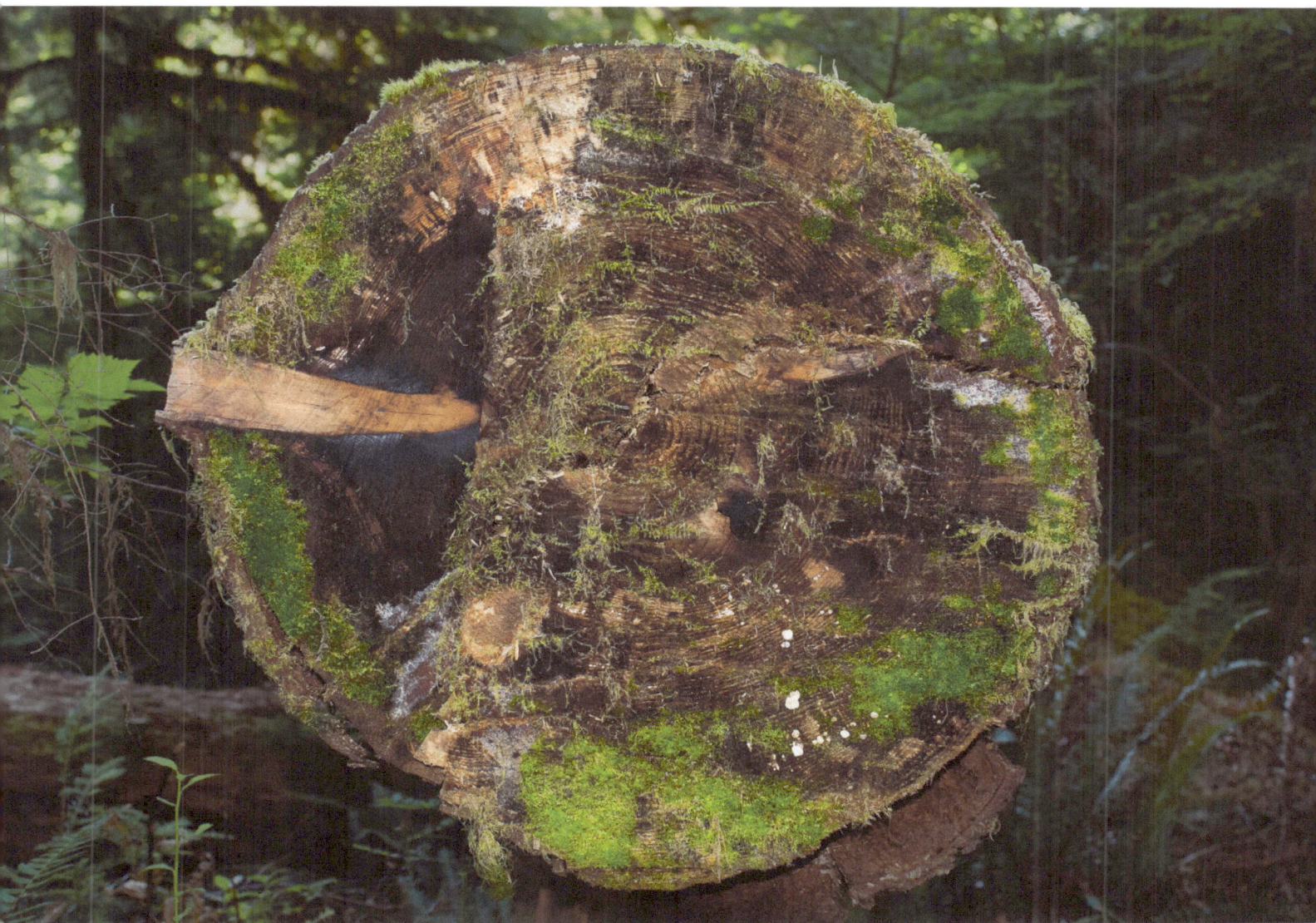

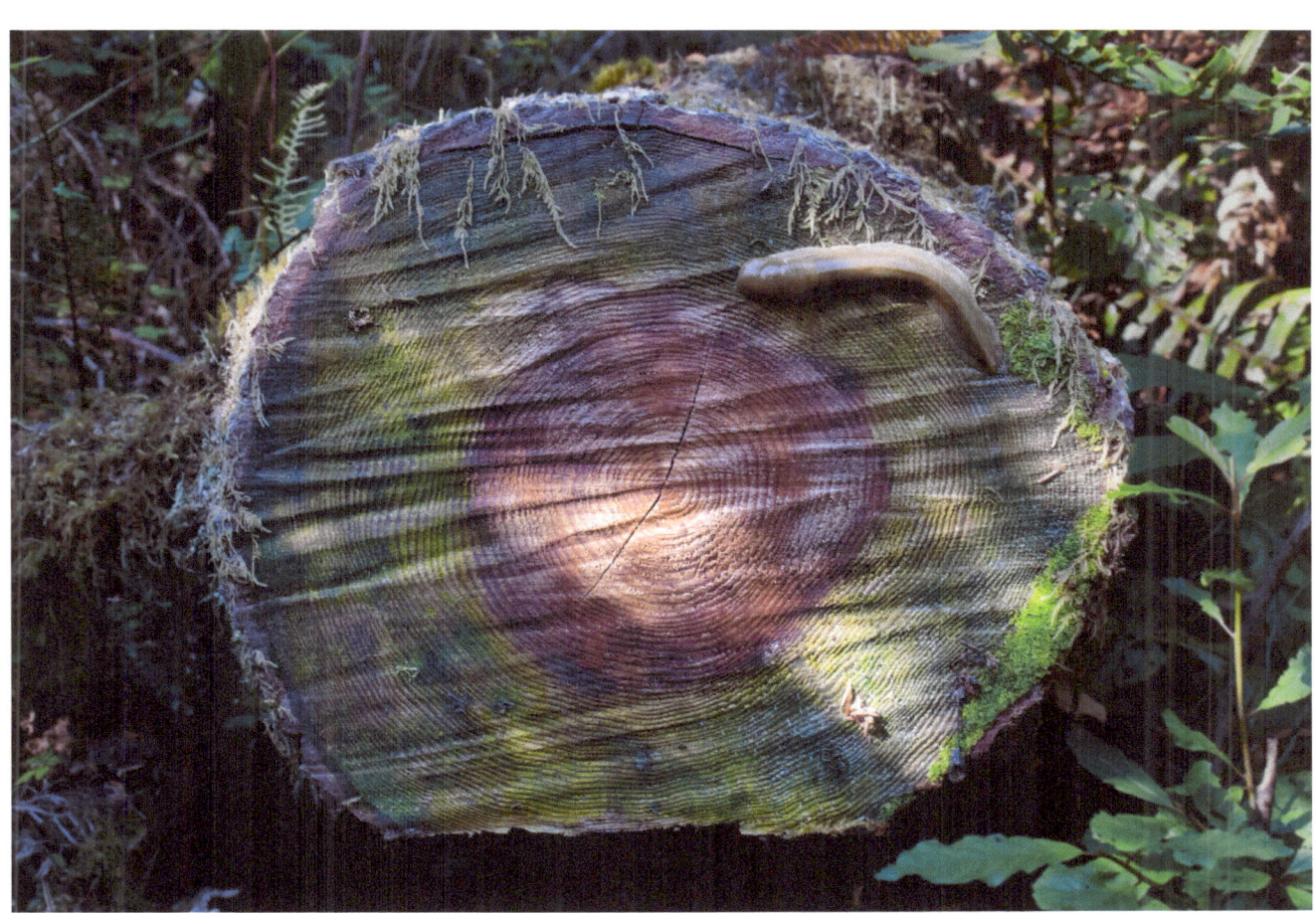

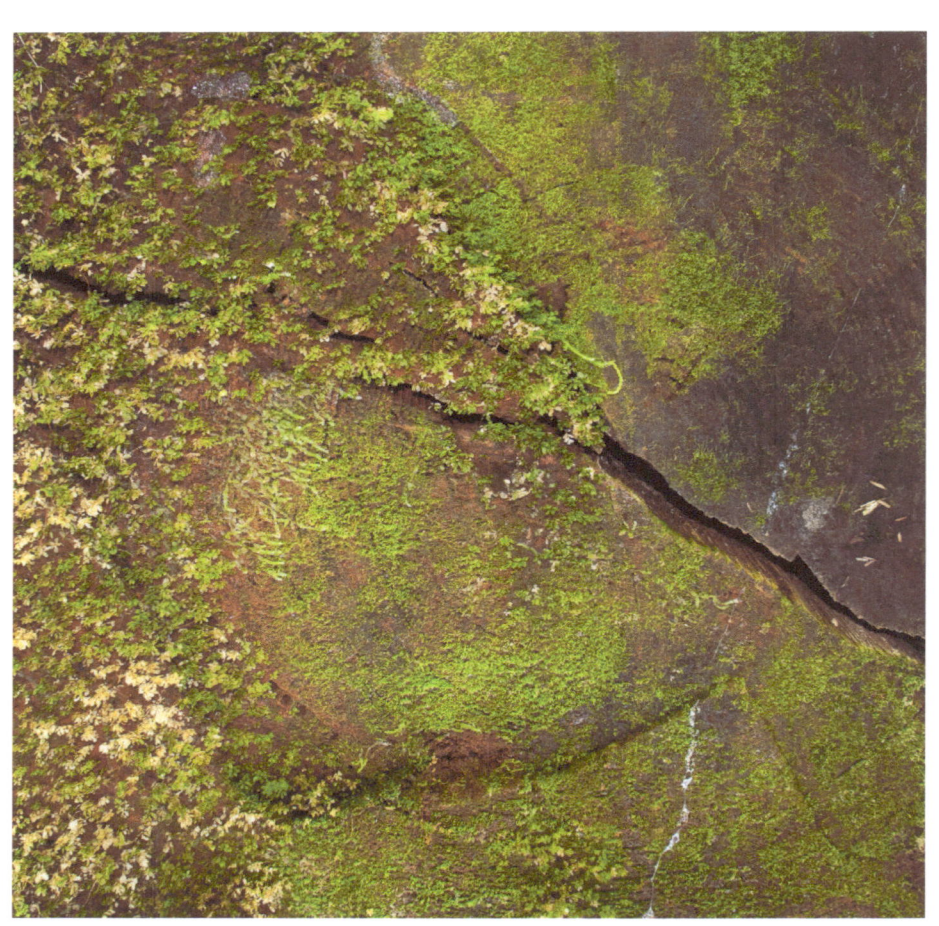

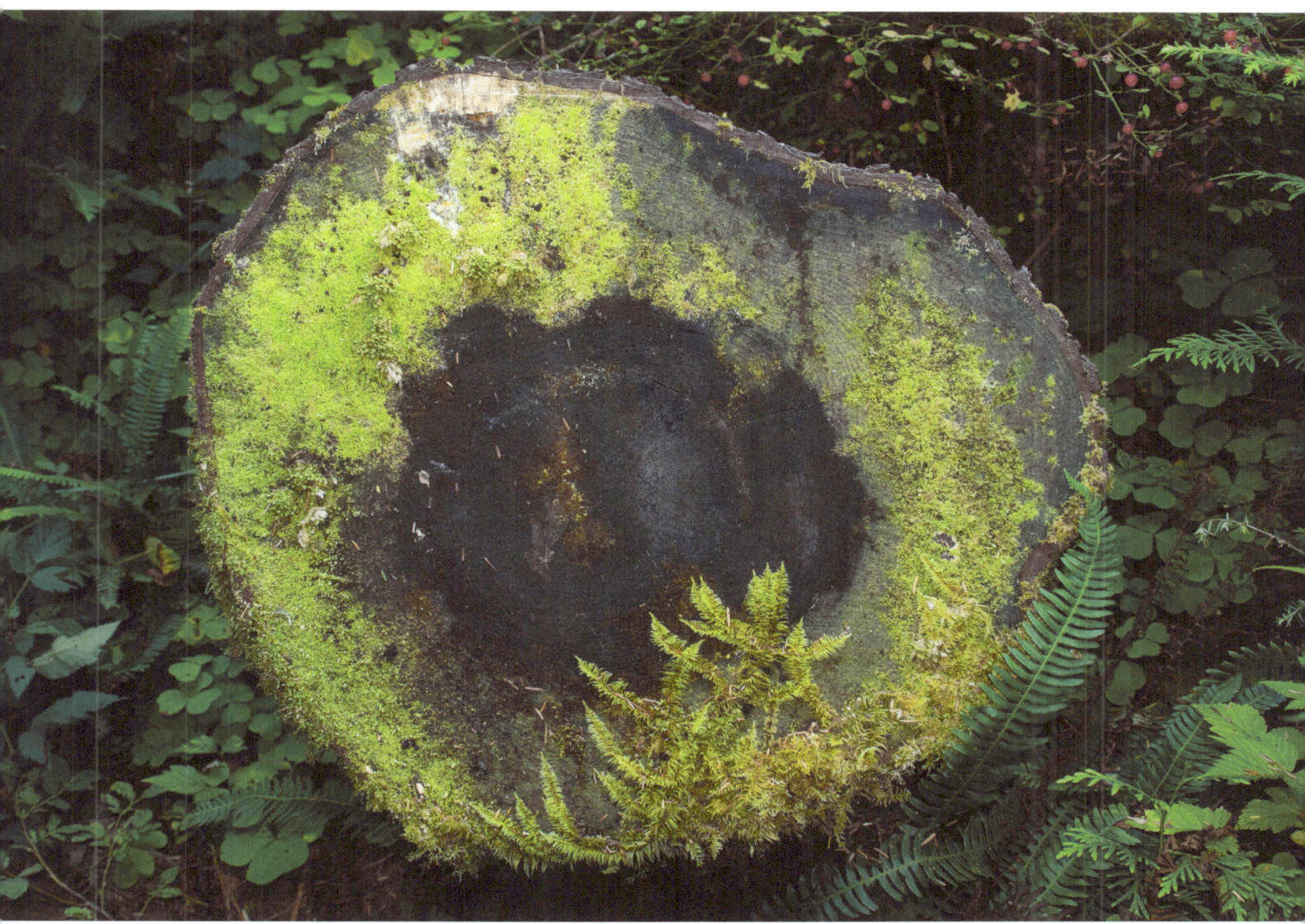

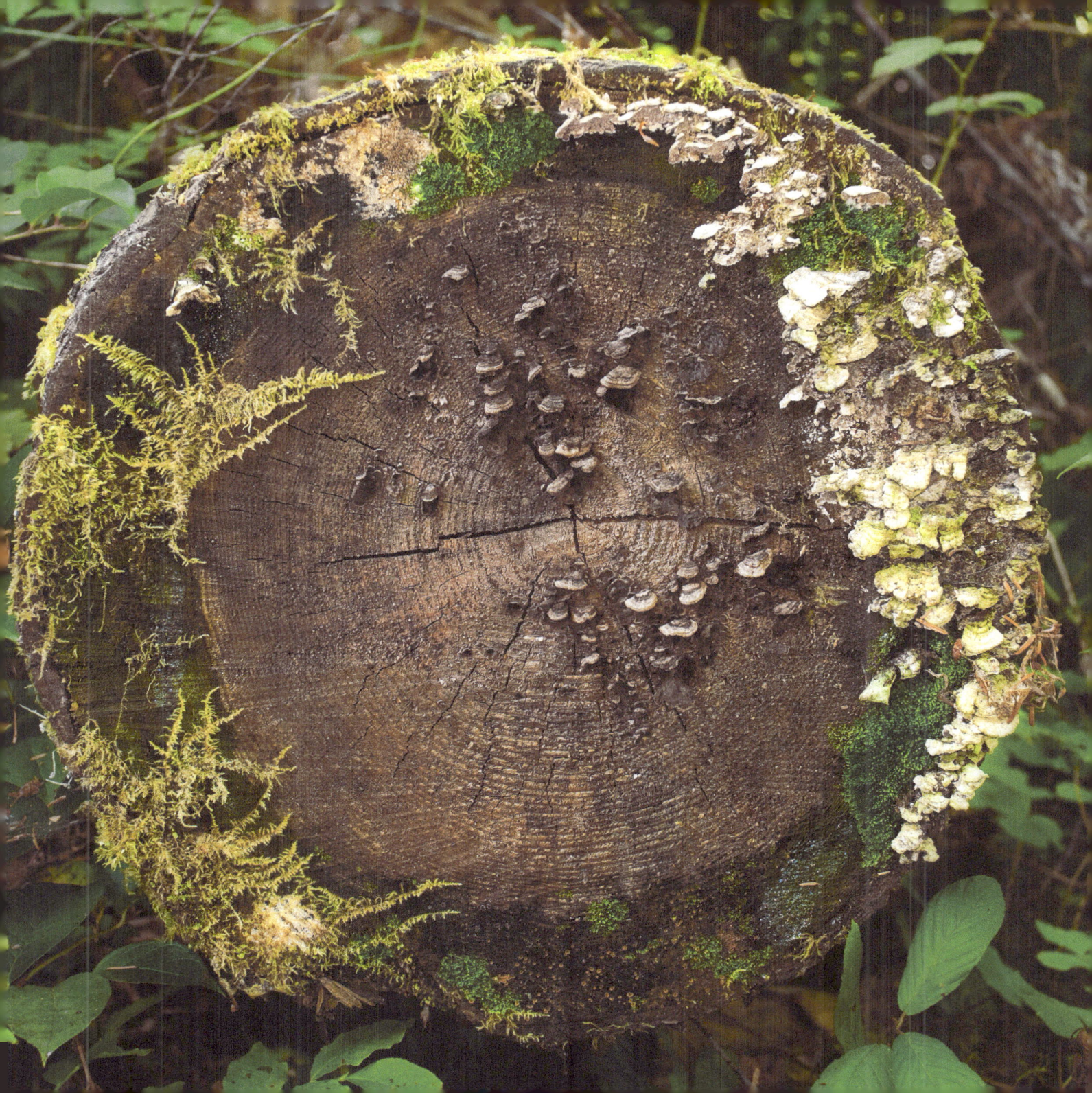

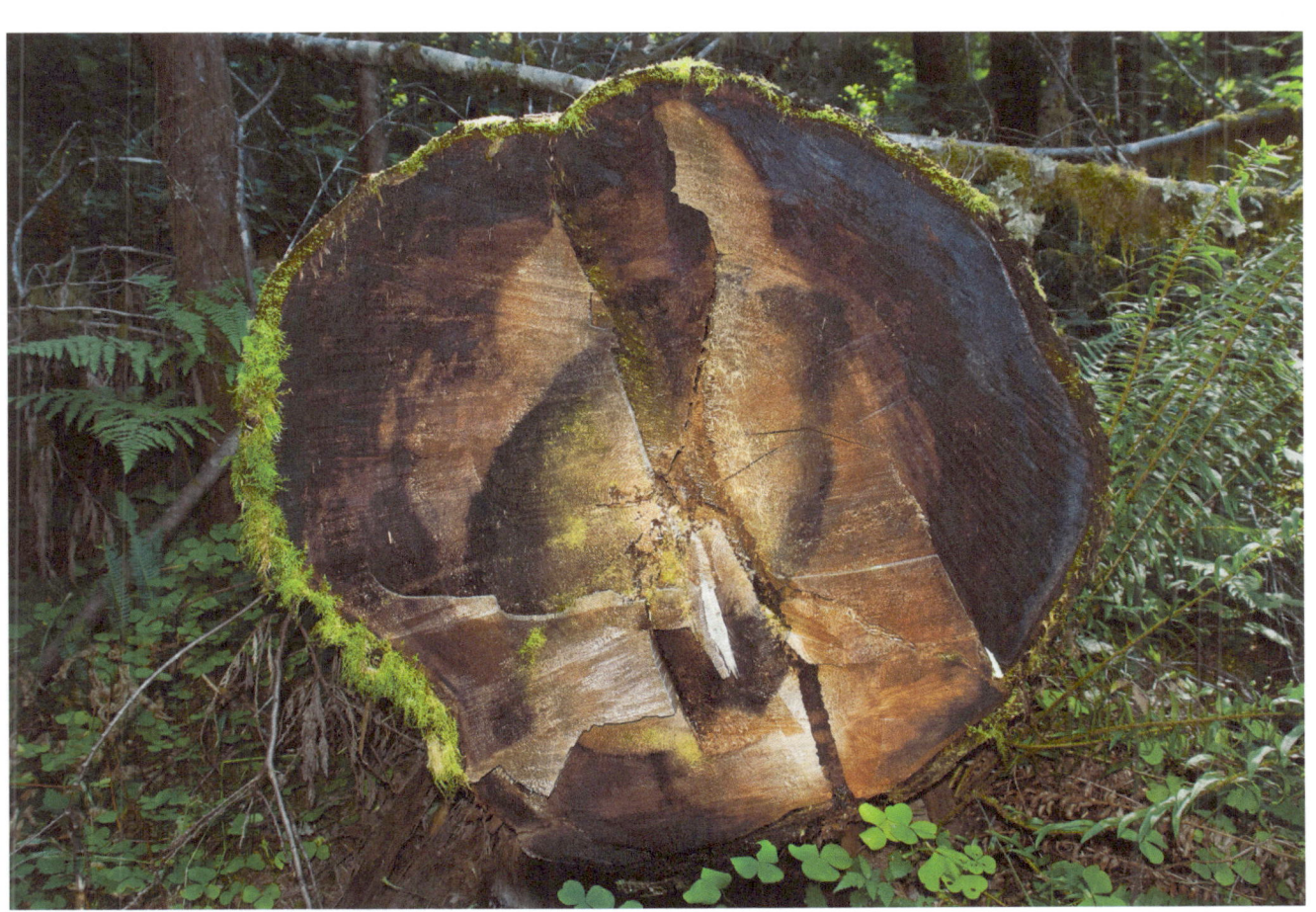

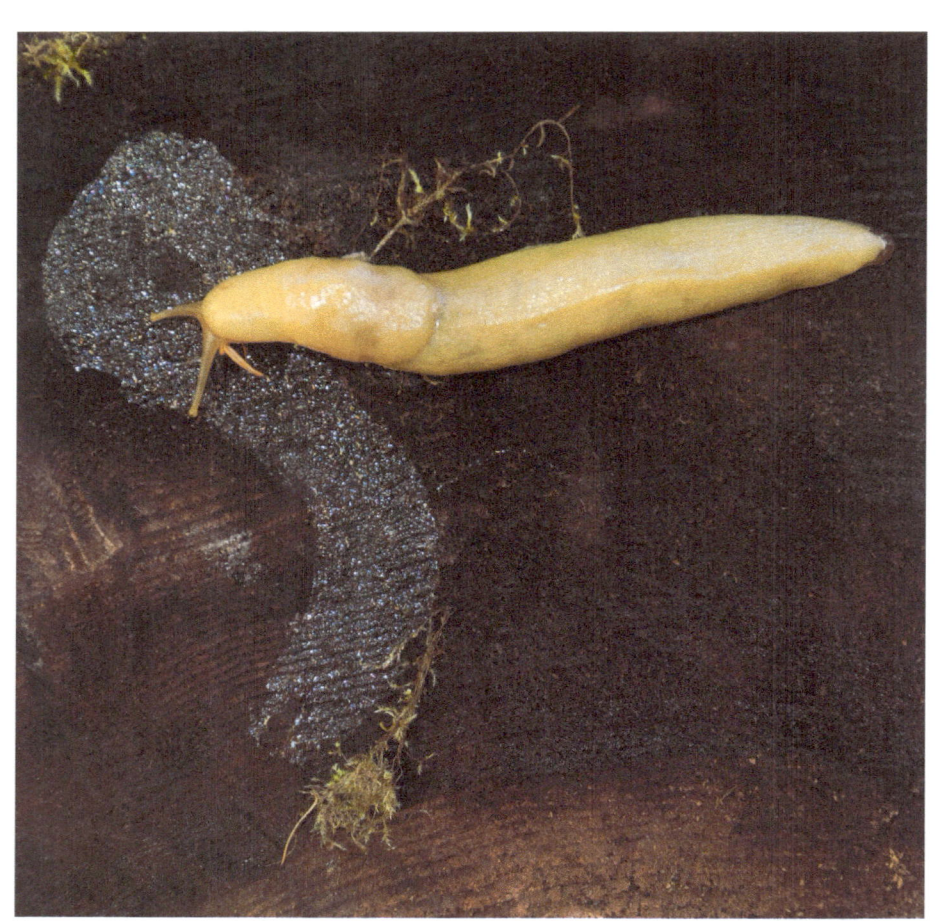

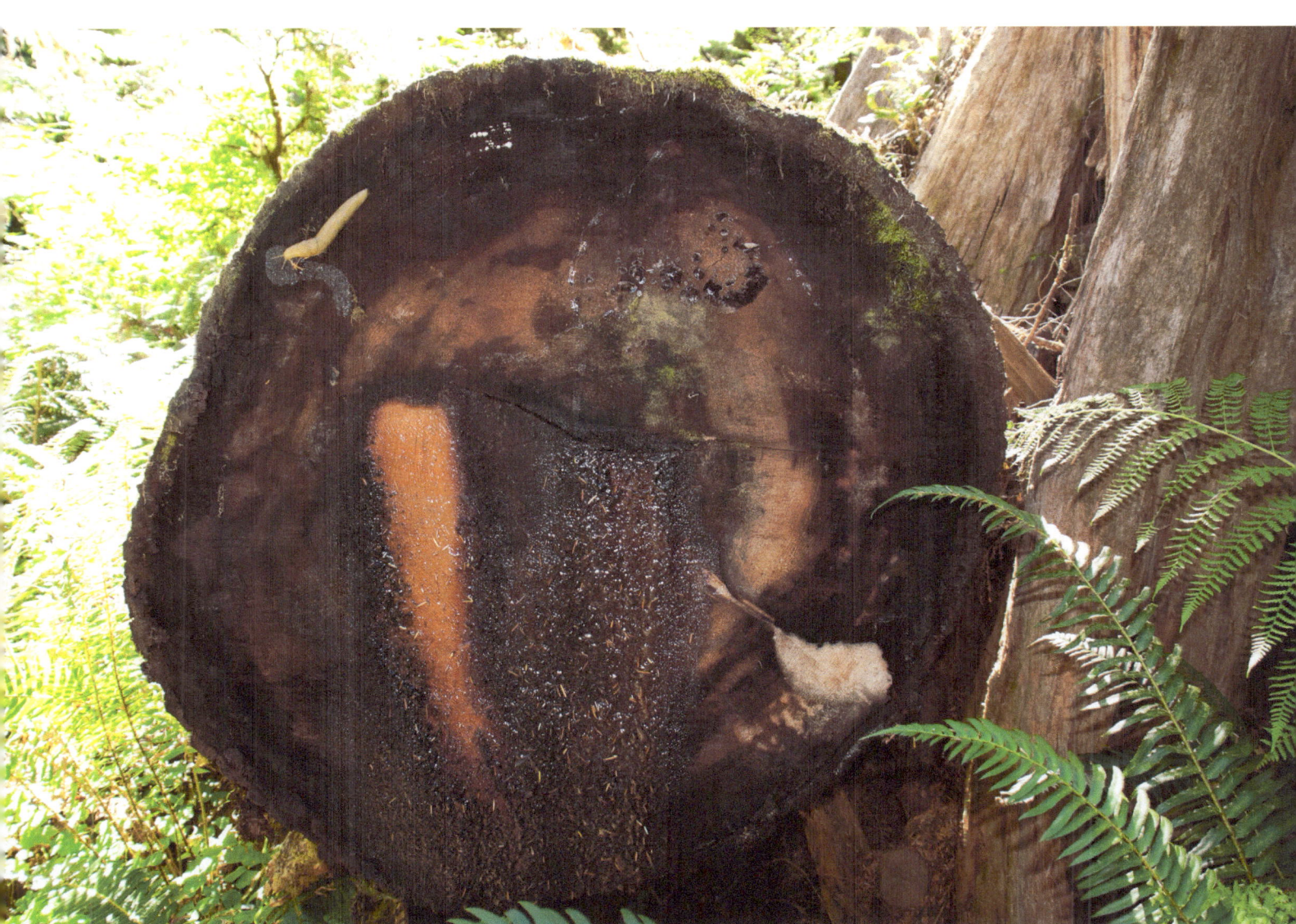

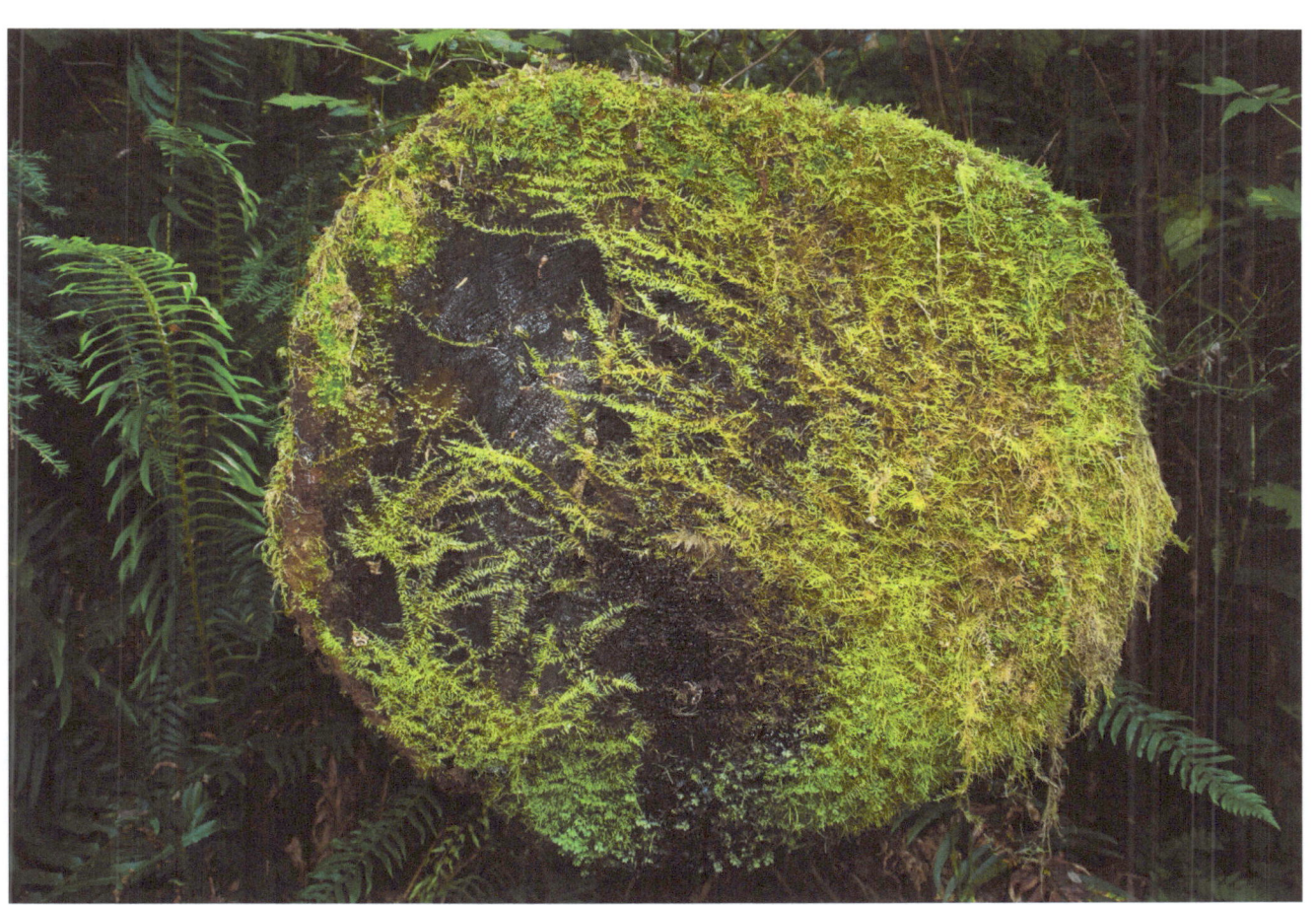

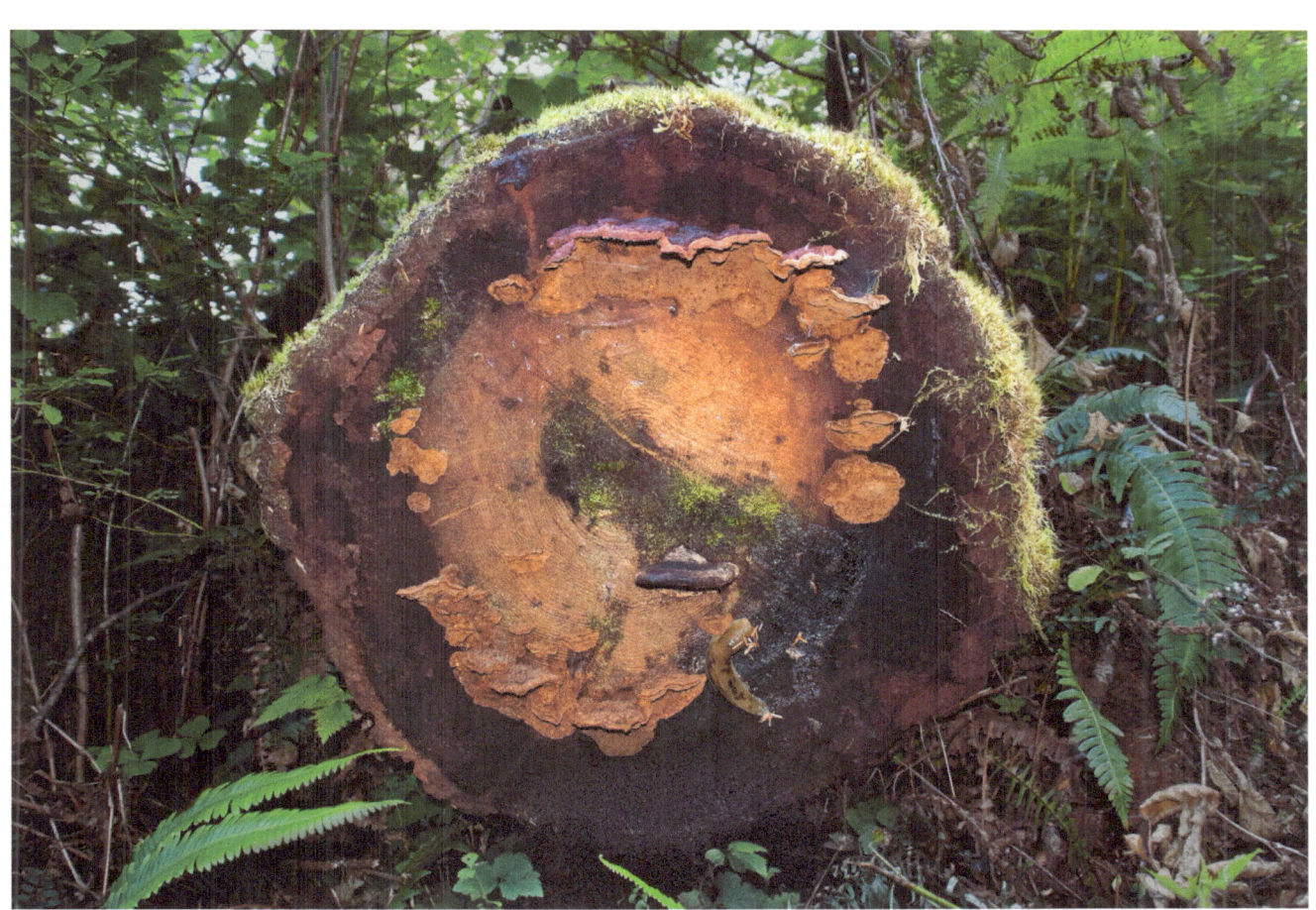

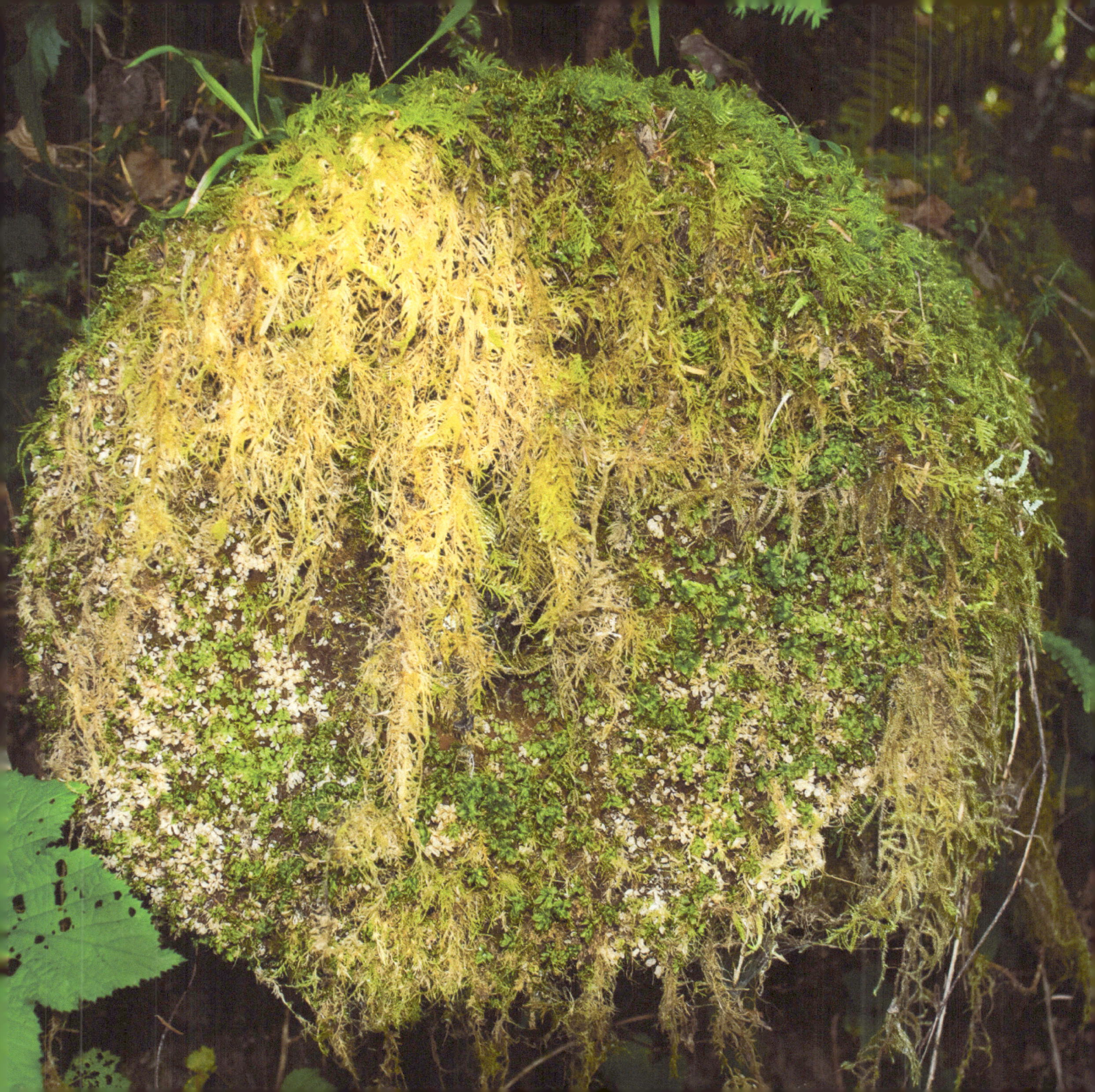

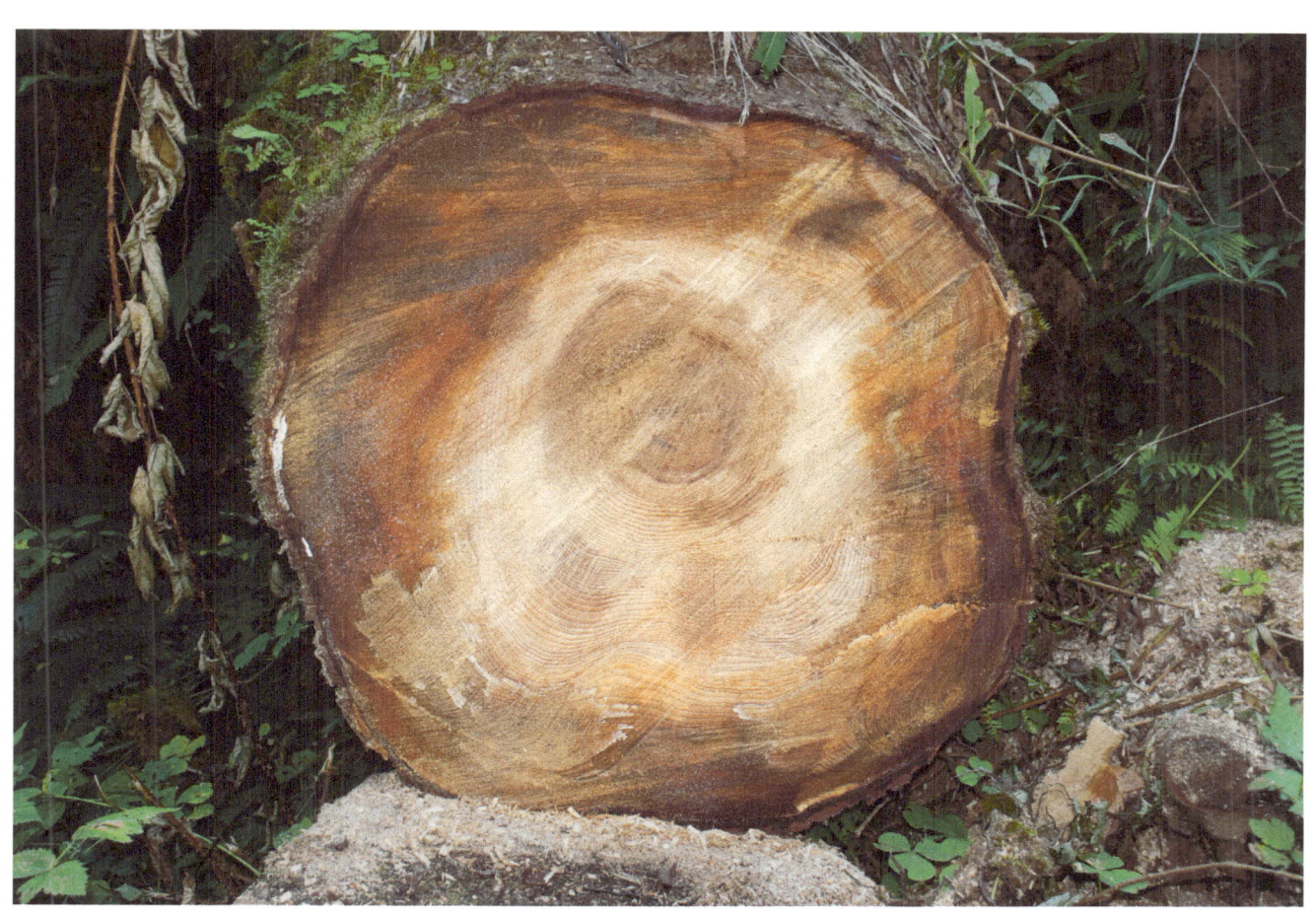

www.ingramcontent.com/pod-product-compliance
Lightning Source LLC
Chambersburg PA
CBHW050414180526
45159CB00005B/2272